The Therapy Reflection Journal

Roslyn Postlewaite, LMSW

DEDICATION

This book is dedicated to my Savior and best friend, Jesus Christ. Thank you for all that you have brought me through and the healing that I get to now share with the world.

My husband, Nico, you've been my biggest supporter and continue to be even now. I love you so very much and am blessed to share this life with you.

Contents

Introduction to Journal: Purpose and Use

Greetings friends,

My name is Roslyn Postlewaite, LMSW. I am the creator and founder of the Therapy as a Christian podcast. I am a Licensed Master Social Worker whose passion is to see others fully heal, along with God, through mental health therapy. My passion for Therapy as a Christian started within my career but catapulted forward when I first began therapy back in 2014. During my on and off time in therapy, I discovered that journaling was my way to reflect and learn about what I was going through and served as my anchor as a way to grow. This consistent reflection was my way of doing the work that my therapist and I worked through. Additionally, having my notes allowed me the opportunity to go back over time and see my progress.

However, throughout my therapy process I haven't been able to really see all of what I've received from each and every session. I wanted to have a specific journal dedicated for therapy that would allow me to keep track of homework, immediate takeaways (so that I did not forget them), and just to get the most out of my sessions. Therapy is challenging in general, but when you're able to see the progress over time and what you can overcome, you show more compassion towards yourself and your growth. This is where the Therapy Reflection Journal came from; this idea came strictly from God and he has laid out the vision for this journal from start to finish. I wanted a way for you to get the most out of therapy whether it is your first therapy session, or you're in the middle of your journey, you can pick this up!

There is no right or wrong way for you to use this journal, but make it a point to take it to every session. If you forget to take it one day, that is okay, just get back into using it at your next session. This isn't about being perfect, but for you to learn and grow within yourself. I would also recommend taking this journal with you into your quiet time with the Lord so that you can reflect, pray, and ask Him for assistance with your therapy experience.

During the time that you use this journal, inform your therapist that you have it. Ask them to hold you accountable in using it, ask them for homework, and some prompts for you to reflect on. Write your thoughts down so that you can easily come back to them. Everything is all in one place specific for you and your journey.

Over the next couple of pages, I will show you how this journal is very simple and easy to use.

Session Page Format: The next page will be what each session page will look like. It is important that you write the **date, mood BEFORE/AFTER session, notes, and homework that your therapist gives you**.

It is vital to keep up with this information throughout your session so that you can get the best use out of the session notes. I added a mood tracker so that you can track how the session made you feel before and after your session. Even though tracking your mood may not seem important, as you go through therapy you will see how certain topics and points of discussion impact your mood. Try to track this consistently.

Additionally, each page will have a section to write down important moments in your session. If it is difficult to focus and write during your session, ask your therapist to list off highlights about 5 minutes before your session ends. Try to be active but if you leave the session and this is blank, that is okay.

Homework usually a term used in therapy to describe topics, assignments, or points that your therapist wants you to think about after your session. This is where the "Post Therapy" and Reflection pages are useful. These specific pages will give you an opportunity to dig deeper into what you and your therapist discussed. Biggest advice: do not neglect your homework. This is how the real work is done so that you are able to really see change happen.

Post therapy: You will see on the next page the "Post Therapy" section. There you will rate your mood following the session and a "What did you learn/Immediate thoughts after session?" All sessions will not be easy and many will be rough, but this will be a place you can write down how your session impacted you. This section is for brief and concise thoughts.

I've included prompts in this section to give you an idea of what you can write in the spaces. However, feel free to use the spaces in any way that you desire.

SESSION PROMPT EXAMPLE:

Session Date: _____

Rate mood **before** session (circle):

```
|—————|—————|—————|—————|
1          2          3          4          5
Sad/Down        Neutral/So-So         Happy/
                                     Optimistic
```

Session Notes: Jot down any words, topics, or notes from your therapy session. Taking notes is helpful in your remembrance of what happened in your session. This section does not have to be full but write down anything that pops out to you during your session. (Examples: quotes, ideas for self-care, things you're currently struggling with, helpful tips you receive, questions that you want to ask but don't want to forget, reflection topics). Let this be your open space to be messy.

_____

_____

_____

_____

_____

_____

_____

_____

_____

_____

Homework/Things to reflect on for next session:

_____

_____

_____

Post therapy: This will be the page where you will write down thoughts or feelings following your session.

Rate mood **after** session (circle):

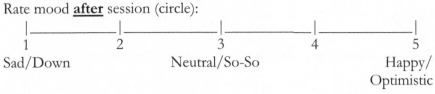

|—————|—————|—————|—————|
1   2   3   4   5
Sad/Down   Neutral/So-So   Happy/
                                       Optimistic

What did you learn? Immediate thoughts after session: (Write down your immediate thoughts. Ex: "this was a hard session." "I found out today that I struggle with boundaries with friends." "I have a lot of un-forgiveness towards my ex." "I'm having a hard time opening up about my abuse." "I realized today that I struggle with confidence." **This space should be short and concise so that you can expound more on your reflection pages.**

_____

_____

_____

_____

_____

Reflection Page Format:

This is the heart of the entire journal. Reflection is an essential part of your therapy journey as it will give you the ability to build your self-awareness and write down how you feel.

Reflection is important, in general, to get the thoughts that you are thinking out of your head but it will also aid in catapulting your understanding further. When you are honest with yourself, you give yourself the opportunity to address the deep rooted issues that you may feel ashamed to share with the people around you. <u>Write that down.</u> It is important to write after your session and throughout this process so that you can see your growth over time.

I believe that the reflection pages will be the pages that you value the most throughout this journal. I've put extra pages in the back of the journal so that you can write and reflect all in one place.

REFLECTION PAGE EXAMPLE:

DATE: _____

Reflection Page:
This is a place where you can work on your homework or reflect
deeper. This page is open for your use to write down anything that you
may feel. Here are some ideas for prompts: What were some of your
thoughts and feelings from your session? What was tough for you to
discuss and open up about? Did you feel enlightened in anyway? How
did it feel to address an area that you may keep closed off from others?
What is a topic that you and your therapist discussed that resonated
with you?

_____

_____

_____

_____

_____

_____

_____

_____

_____

_____

_____

_____

_____

_____

_____

Now that we've covered what this journal will entail. I know you will enjoy this journey. Best wishes! You can do it! You've taken the first step by starting, be proud of yourself.

Session Date: _____

Rate mood **<u>before</u>** session (circle):

|——————|——————|——————|——————|
1   2   3   4   5
Sad/Down   Neutral/So-So   Happy/
                                                  Optimistic

Session Notes: Jot down any words, topics, or notes from your therapy session. Taking notes is helpful in your remembrance of what happened in your session. This section does not have to be full but write down anything that pops out to you during your session. (Examples: quotes, ideas for self-care, things you're currently struggling with, helpful tips you receive, questions that you want to ask but don't want to forget, reflection topics). Let this be your open space to be messy.

_____

_____

_____

_____

_____

_____

_____

_____

_____

_____

Homework/Things to reflect on for next session:

_____

_____

_____

Post therapy: This will be the page where you will write down thoughts or feelings following your session.

Rate mood **after** session (circle):

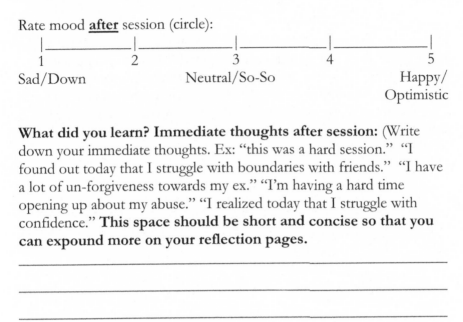

|—————|—————|—————|—————|
1   2   3   4   5
Sad/Down   Neutral/So-So   Happy/
                                                                      Optimistic

What did you learn? Immediate thoughts after session: (Write down your immediate thoughts. Ex: "this was a hard session." "I found out today that I struggle with boundaries with friends." "I have a lot of un-forgiveness towards my ex." "I'm having a hard time opening up about my abuse." "I realized today that I struggle with confidence." **This space should be short and concise so that you can expound more on your reflection pages.**

———————————————————————————

———————————————————————————

———————————————————————————

———————————————————————————

———————————————————————————

Reflection Page:

DATE: _____

This is a place where you can work on your homework or reflect deeper. This page is open for your use to write down anything that you may feel. Here are some ideas for prompts: What were some of your thoughts and feelings from your session? What was tough for you to discuss and open up about? Did you feel enlightened in anyway? How did it feel to address an area that you may keep closed off from others? What is a topic that you and your therapist discussed that resonated with you?

_____

_____

_____

_____

_____

_____

_____

_____

_____

_____

_____

_____

_____

_____

_____

_____

Session Date: _____

Rate mood **before** session (circle):

|——————|——————|——————|——————|
1   2   3   4   5

Sad/Down   Neutral/So-So   Happy/
                                                       Optimistic

Session Notes: Jot down any words, topics, or notes from your therapy session. Taking notes is helpful in your remembrance of what happened in your session. This section does not have to be full but write down anything that pops out to you during your session. (Examples: quotes, ideas for self-care, things you're currently struggling with, helpful tips you receive, questions that you want to ask but don't want to forget, reflection topics). Let this be your open space to be messy.

_____

_____

_____

_____

_____

_____

_____

_____

_____

_____

Homework/Things to reflect on for next session:

_____

_____

_____

Post therapy: This will be the page where you will write down thoughts or feelings following your session.

Rate mood **<u>after</u>** session (circle):

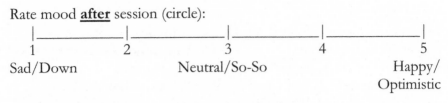

|————————|————————|————————|————————|
1   2   3   4   5

Sad/Down   Neutral/So-So   Happy/
                                                                    Optimistic

What did you learn? Immediate thoughts after session: (Write down your immediate thoughts. Ex: "this was a hard session." "I found out today that I struggle with boundaries with friends." "I have a lot of un-forgiveness towards my ex." "I'm having a hard time opening up about my abuse." "I realized today that I struggle with confidence." **This space should be short and concise so that you can expound more on your reflection pages.**

———————————————————————————————————

———————————————————————————————————

———————————————————————————————————

———————————————————————————————————

———————————————————————————————————

Reflection Page:

DATE: _____

This is a place where you can work on your homework or reflect deeper. This page is open for your use to write down anything that you may feel. Here are some ideas for prompts: What were some of your thoughts and feelings from your session? What was tough for you to discuss and open up about? Did you feel enlightened in anyway? How did it feel to address an area that you may keep closed off from others? What is a topic that you and your therapist discussed that resonated with you?

_____

_____

_____

_____

_____

_____

_____

_____

_____

_____

_____

_____

_____

_____

_____

_____

_____

_____

Session Date: _____

Rate mood **before** session (circle):

|————————|————————|————————|————————|
1   2   3   4   5

Sad/Down   Neutral/So-So   Happy/
                                                  Optimistic

Session Notes: Jot down any words, topics, or notes from your therapy session. Taking notes is helpful in your remembrance of what happened in your session. This section does not have to be full but write down anything that pops out to you during your session. (Examples: quotes, ideas for self-care, things you're currently struggling with, helpful tips you receive, questions that you want to ask but don't want to forget, reflection topics). Let this be your open space to be messy.

_____

_____

_____

_____

_____

_____

_____

_____

_____

_____

Homework/Things to reflect on for next session:

_____

_____

_____

Post therapy: This will be the page where you will write down thoughts or feelings following your session.

Rate mood <u>**after**</u> session (circle):

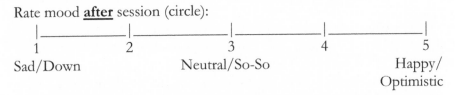

|——————|——————|——————|——————|
1   2   3   4   5
Sad/Down   Neutral/So-So   Happy/
                                     Optimistic

What did you learn? Immediate thoughts after session: (Write down your immediate thoughts. Ex: "this was a hard session." "I found out today that I struggle with boundaries with friends." "I have a lot of un-forgiveness towards my ex." "I'm having a hard time opening up about my abuse." "I realized today that I struggle with confidence." **This space should be short and concise so that you can expound more on your reflection pages.**

_____

_____

_____

_____

_____

Reflection Page:

DATE: _____

This is a place where you can work on your homework or reflect
deeper. This page is open for your use to write down anything that you
may feel. Here are some ideas for prompts: What were some of your
thoughts and feelings from your session? What was tough for you to
discuss and open up about? Did you feel enlightened in anyway? How
did it feel to address an area that you may keep closed off from others?
What is a topic that you and your therapist discussed that resonated
with you?

_____

_____

_____

_____

_____

_____

_____

_____

_____

_____

_____

_____

_____

_____

_____

_____

Session Date: _____

Rate mood **before** session (circle):

|————————|————————|————————|————————|
1   2   3   4   5
Sad/Down   Neutral/So-So   Happy/
                                                        Optimistic

Session Notes: Jot down any words, topics, or notes from your therapy session. Taking notes is helpful in your remembrance of what happened in your session. This section does not have to be full but write down anything that pops out to you during your session. (Examples: quotes, ideas for self-care, things you're currently struggling with, helpful tips you receive, questions that you want to ask but don't want to forget, reflection topics). Let this be your open space to be messy.

_____

_____

_____

_____

_____

_____

_____

_____

_____

_____

Homework/Things to reflect on for next session:

_____

_____

_____

Post therapy: This will be the page where you will write down thoughts or feelings following your session.

Rate mood **after** session (circle):

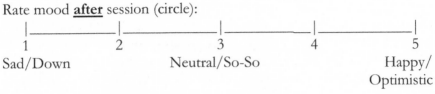

|——————|——————|——————|——————|
1   2   3   4   5
Sad/Down   Neutral/So-So   Happy/
                                                 Optimistic

What did you learn? Immediate thoughts after session: (Write down your immediate thoughts. Ex: "this was a hard session." "I found out today that I struggle with boundaries with friends." "I have a lot of un-forgiveness towards my ex." "I'm having a hard time opening up about my abuse." "I realized today that I struggle with confidence." **This space should be short and concise so that you can expound more on your reflection pages.**

_____

_____

_____

_____

_____

Reflection Page:

DATE: _____

This is a place where you can work on your homework or reflect deeper. This page is open for your use to write down anything that you may feel. Here are some ideas for prompts: What were some of your thoughts and feelings from your session? What was tough for you to discuss and open up about? Did you feel enlightened in anyway? How did it feel to address an area that you may keep closed off from others? What is a topic that you and your therapist discussed that resonated with you?

_____

_____

_____

_____

_____

_____

_____

_____

_____

_____

_____

_____

_____

_____

_____

_____

Session Date: _____

Rate mood **before** session (circle):

|————————|————————|————————|————————|
1   2   3   4   5
Sad/Down   Neutral/So-So   Happy/
                                               Optimistic

Session Notes: Jot down any words, topics, or notes from your therapy session. Taking notes is helpful in your remembrance of what happened in your session. This section does not have to be full but write down anything that pops out to you during your session. (Examples: quotes, ideas for self-care, things you're currently struggling with, helpful tips you receive, questions that you want to ask but don't want to forget, reflection topics). Let this be your open space to be messy.

_____

_____

_____

_____

_____

_____

_____

_____

_____

_____

Homework/Things to reflect on for next session:

_____

_____

_____

Post therapy: This will be the page where you will write down thoughts or feelings following your session.

Rate mood **after** session (circle):

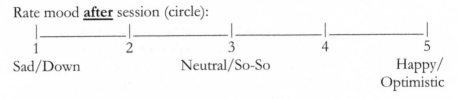

1
Sad/Down

2

3
Neutral/So-So

4

5
Happy/
Optimistic

What did you learn? Immediate thoughts after session: (Write down your immediate thoughts. Ex: "this was a hard session." "I found out today that I struggle with boundaries with friends." "I have a lot of un-forgiveness towards my ex." "I'm having a hard time opening up about my abuse." "I realized today that I struggle with confidence." **This space should be short and concise so that you can expound more on your reflection pages.**

_____

_____

_____

_____

_____

Reflection Page:

DATE: _____

This is a place where you can work on your homework or reflect deeper. This page is open for your use to write down anything that you may feel. Here are some ideas for prompts: What were some of your thoughts and feelings from your session? What was tough for you to discuss and open up about? Did you feel enlightened in anyway? How did it feel to address an area that you may keep closed off from others? What is a topic that you and your therapist discussed that resonated with you?

_____

_____

_____

_____

_____

_____

_____

_____

_____

_____

_____

_____

_____

_____

_____

_____

_____

Session Date: _____

Rate mood **before** session (circle):

|———————|———————|———————|———————|
1   2   3   4   5
Sad/Down   Neutral/So-So   Happy/
                                                        Optimistic

Session Notes: Jot down any words, topics, or notes from your therapy session. Taking notes is helpful in your remembrance of what happened in your session. This section does not have to be full but write down anything that pops out to you during your session. (Examples: quotes, ideas for self-care, things you're currently struggling with, helpful tips you receive, questions that you want to ask but don't want to forget, reflection topics). Let this be your open space to be messy.

_____

_____

_____

_____

_____

_____

_____

_____

_____

Homework/Things to reflect on for next session:

_____

_____

_____

Post therapy: This will be the page where you will write down thoughts or feelings following your session.

Rate mood **after** session (circle):

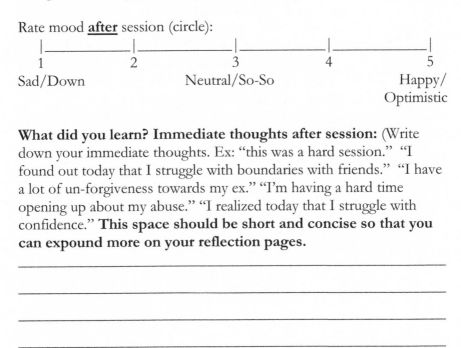

|————————|————————|————————|————————|
1   2   3   4   5

Sad/Down   Neutral/So-So   Happy/
Optimistic

What did you learn? Immediate thoughts after session: (Write down your immediate thoughts. Ex: "this was a hard session." "I found out today that I struggle with boundaries with friends." "I have a lot of un-forgiveness towards my ex." "I'm having a hard time opening up about my abuse." "I realized today that I struggle with confidence." **This space should be short and concise so that you can expound more on your reflection pages.**

_____

_____

_____

_____

_____

Reflection Page:

DATE: _____

This is a place where you can work on your homework or reflect deeper. This page is open for your use to write down anything that you may feel. Here are some ideas for prompts: What were some of your thoughts and feelings from your session? What was tough for you to discuss and open up about? Did you feel enlightened in anyway? How did it feel to address an area that you may keep closed off from others? What is a topic that you and your therapist discussed that resonated with you?

_____

_____

_____

_____

_____

_____

_____

_____

_____

_____

_____

_____

_____

_____

_____

_____

Session Date: _____

Rate mood **before** session (circle):

|—————|—————|—————|—————|
1   2   3   4   5
Sad/Down   Neutral/So-So   Happy/
                                                 Optimistic

Session Notes: Jot down any words, topics, or notes from your therapy session. Taking notes is helpful in your remembrance of what happened in your session. This section does not have to be full but write down anything that pops out to you during your session. (Examples: quotes, ideas for self-care, things you're currently struggling with, helpful tips you receive, questions that you want to ask but don't want to forget, reflection topics). Let this be your open space to be messy.

_____

_____

_____

_____

_____

_____

_____

_____

_____

_____

Homework/Things to reflect on for next session:

_____

_____

_____

Post therapy: This will be the page where you will write down thoughts or feelings following your session.

Rate mood **<u>after</u>** session (circle):

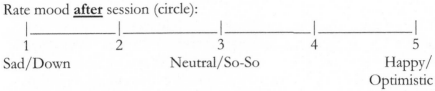

| 1 | 2 | 3 | 4 | 5 |
| Sad/Down | | Neutral/So-So | | Happy/Optimistic |

What did you learn? Immediate thoughts after session: (Write down your immediate thoughts. Ex: "this was a hard session." "I found out today that I struggle with boundaries with friends." "I have a lot of un-forgiveness towards my ex." "I'm having a hard time opening up about my abuse." "I realized today that I struggle with confidence." **This space should be short and concise so that you can expound more on your reflection pages.**

_____

_____

_____

_____

_____

Reflection Page:

DATE: _____

This is a place where you can work on your homework or reflect deeper. This page is open for your use to write down anything that you may feel. Here are some ideas for prompts: What were some of your thoughts and feelings from your session? What was tough for you to discuss and open up about? Did you feel enlightened in anyway? How did it feel to address an area that you may keep closed off from others? What is a topic that you and your therapist discussed that resonated with you?

_____

_____

_____

_____

_____

_____

_____

_____

_____

_____

_____

_____

_____

_____

_____

_____

_____

Session Date: _____

Rate mood **before** session (circle):

|—————|—————|—————|—————|
1   2   3   4   5
Sad/Down   Neutral/So-So   Happy/
                                                Optimistic

Session Notes: Jot down any words, topics, or notes from your therapy session. Taking notes is helpful in your remembrance of what happened in your session. This section does not have to be full but write down anything that pops out to you during your session. (Examples: quotes, ideas for self-care, things you're currently struggling with, helpful tips you receive, questions that you want to ask but don't want to forget, reflection topics). Let this be your open space to be messy.

_____

_____

_____

_____

_____

_____

_____

_____

_____

_____

Homework/Things to reflect on for next session:

_____

_____

_____

Post therapy: This will be the page where you will write down thoughts or feelings following your session.

Rate mood **after** session (circle):

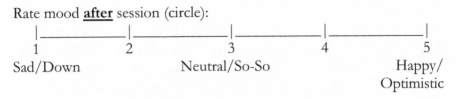

| |_____| |_____| |_____| |_____| |
1   2   3   4   5
Sad/Down   Neutral/So-So   Happy/
                                                                       Optimistic

What did you learn? Immediate thoughts after session: (Write down your immediate thoughts. Ex: "this was a hard session." "I found out today that I struggle with boundaries with friends." "I have a lot of un-forgiveness towards my ex." "I'm having a hard time opening up about my abuse." "I realized today that I struggle with confidence." **This space should be short and concise so that you can expound more on your reflection pages.**

_____

_____

_____

_____

_____

Reflection Page:

DATE: _____

This is a place where you can work on your homework or reflect deeper. This page is open for your use to write down anything that you may feel. Here are some ideas for prompts: What were some of your thoughts and feelings from your session? What was tough for you to discuss and open up about? Did you feel enlightened in anyway? How did it feel to address an area that you may keep closed off from others? What is a topic that you and your therapist discussed that resonated with you?

_____

_____

_____

_____

_____

_____

_____

_____

_____

_____

_____

_____

_____

_____

_____

_____

Session Date: _____

Rate mood **before** session (circle):

|————————|————————|————————|————————|
1   2   3   4   5
Sad/Down   Neutral/So-So   Happy/
                                                     Optimistic

Session Notes: Jot down any words, topics, or notes from your therapy session. Taking notes is helpful in your remembrance of what happened in your session. This section does not have to be full but write down anything that pops out to you during your session. (Examples: quotes, ideas for self-care, things you're currently struggling with, helpful tips you receive, questions that you want to ask but don't want to forget, reflection topics). Let this be your open space to be messy.

_____

_____

_____

_____

_____

_____

_____

_____

_____

Homework/Things to reflect on for next session:

_____

_____

_____

Post therapy: This will be the page where you will write down thoughts or feelings following your session.

Rate mood **after** session (circle):

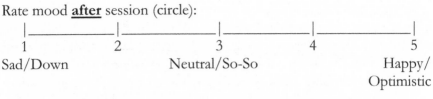

|—————|—————|—————|—————|
1   2   3   4   5
Sad/Down   Neutral/So-So   Happy/
                                                Optimistic

What did you learn? Immediate thoughts after session: (Write down your immediate thoughts. Ex: "this was a hard session." "I found out today that I struggle with boundaries with friends." "I have a lot of un-forgiveness towards my ex." "I'm having a hard time opening up about my abuse." "I realized today that I struggle with confidence." **This space should be short and concise so that you can expound more on your reflection pages.**

_____

_____

_____

_____

_____

Reflection Page:

DATE: _____

This is a place where you can work on your homework or reflect deeper. This page is open for your use to write down anything that you may feel. Here are some ideas for prompts: What were some of your thoughts and feelings from your session? What was tough for you to discuss and open up about? Did you feel enlightened in anyway? How did it feel to address an area that you may keep closed off from others? What is a topic that you and your therapist discussed that resonated with you?

_____

_____

_____

_____

_____

_____

_____

_____

_____

_____

_____

_____

_____

_____

_____

_____

_____

Session Date: _____

Rate mood **before** session (circle):

|—————|—————|—————|—————|
1   2   3   4   5
Sad/Down   Neutral/So-So   Happy/
                                                   Optimistic

Session Notes: Jot down any words, topics, or notes from your therapy session. Taking notes is helpful in your remembrance of what happened in your session. This section does not have to be full but write down anything that pops out to you during your session. (Examples: quotes, ideas for self-care, things you're currently struggling with, helpful tips you receive, questions that you want to ask but don't want to forget, reflection topics). Let this be your open space to be messy.

_____

_____

_____

_____

_____

_____

_____

_____

_____

_____

Homework/Things to reflect on for next session:

_____

_____

_____

Post therapy: This will be the page where you will write down thoughts or feelings following your session.

Rate mood **<u>after</u>** session (circle):

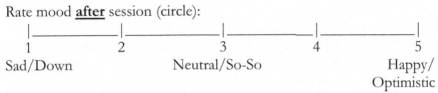

| \|————————\|————————\|————————\|————————\| |
| 1   2   3   4   5 |

1   2   3   4   5
Sad/Down   Neutral/So-So   Happy/
                                                                    Optimistic

What did you learn? Immediate thoughts after session: (Write down your immediate thoughts. Ex: "this was a hard session." "I found out today that I struggle with boundaries with friends." "I have a lot of un-forgiveness towards my ex." "I'm having a hard time opening up about my abuse." "I realized today that I struggle with confidence." **This space should be short and concise so that you can expound more on your reflection pages.**

_____

_____

_____

_____

_____

Reflection Page:

DATE: _____

This is a place where you can work on your homework or reflect deeper. This page is open for your use to write down anything that you may feel. Here are some ideas for prompts: What were some of your thoughts and feelings from your session? What was tough for you to discuss and open up about? Did you feel enlightened in anyway? How did it feel to address an area that you may keep closed off from others? What is a topic that you and your therapist discussed that resonated with you?

_____

_____

_____

_____

_____

_____

_____

_____

_____

_____

_____

_____

_____

_____

_____

_____

Session Date: _____

Rate mood **before** session (circle):

|————————|————————|————————|————————|
1   2   3   4   5
Sad/Down   Neutral/So-So   Happy/
                                                               Optimistic

Session Notes: Jot down any words, topics, or notes from your therapy session.

_____

_____

_____

_____

_____

_____

_____

_____

_____

_____

_____

_____

_____

_____

_____

Homework/Things to reflect on for next session:

_____

_____

_____

58

Post therapy:

Rate mood **after** session (circle):

|———————|———————|———————|———————|
1   2   3   4   5
Sad/Down   Neutral/So-So   Happy/
                                                  Optimistic

What did you learn? Immediate thoughts after session:

_____

_____

_____

_____

_____

Reflection Page:

DATE: _____

_____
_____
_____
_____
_____
_____
_____
_____
_____
_____
_____
_____
_____
_____
_____
_____
_____
_____
_____
_____
_____
_____
_____
_____

Session Date: _____

Rate mood **before** session (circle):

|—————|—————|—————|—————|
1   2   3   4   5
Sad/Down   Neutral/So-So   Happy/
                                                            Optimistic

Session Notes: Jot down any words, topics, or notes from your therapy session.

_____

_____

_____

_____

_____

_____

_____

_____

_____

_____

_____

_____

_____

_____

_____

_____

Homework/Things to reflect on for next session:

_____

_____

_____

Post therapy:

Rate mood **after** session (circle):

| _____ | _____ | _____ | _____ |
1   2   3   4   5

Sad/Down   Neutral/So-So   Happy/
Optimistic

What did you learn? Immediate thoughts after session:

_____

_____

_____

_____

_____

Reflection Page:

DATE: _____

Session Date: _____

Rate mood **before** session (circle):

|—————|—————|—————|—————|
1   2   3   4   5
Sad/Down   Neutral/So-So   Happy/
Optimistic

Session Notes: Jot down any words, topics, or notes from your therapy session.

_____

_____

_____

_____

_____

_____

_____

_____

_____

_____

_____

_____

_____

_____

_____

Homework/Things to reflect on for next session:

_____

_____

_____

Post therapy:

Rate mood **after** session (circle):

```
|_____|_____|_____|_____|
1           2           3           4           5
Sad/Down            Neutral/So-So           Happy/
                                            Optimistic
```

What did you learn? Immediate thoughts after session:

_____

_____

_____

_____

_____

Reflection Page:

DATE: _____

_____
_____
_____
_____
_____
_____
_____
_____
_____
_____
_____
_____
_____
_____
_____
_____
_____
_____
_____
_____
_____
_____
_____

Session Date: _____

Rate mood **before** session (circle):

|—————|—————|—————|—————|
1   2   3   4   5
Sad/Down   Neutral/So-So   Happy/
                                                  Optimistic

Session Notes: Jot down any words, topics, or notes from your therapy session.

_____

_____

_____

_____

_____

_____

_____

_____

_____

_____

_____

_____

_____

_____

_____

_____

Homework/Things to reflect on for next session:

_____

_____

_____

Post therapy:

Rate mood **after** session (circle):

|———————|———————|———————|———————|
1   2   3   4   5

Sad/Down   Neutral/So-So   Happy/
                                                            Optimistic

What did you learn? Immediate thoughts after session:

_____

_____

_____

_____

_____

Reflection Page:

DATE: _____

_____
_____
_____
_____
_____
_____
_____
_____
_____
_____
_____
_____
_____
_____
_____
_____
_____
_____
_____
_____
_____
_____
_____
_____

Session Date: _____

Rate mood **before** session (circle):

|—————|—————|—————|—————|
1   2   3   4   5
Sad/Down   Neutral/So-So   Happy/
Optimistic

Session Notes: Jot down any words, topics, or notes from your therapy session.

_____

_____

_____

_____

_____

_____

_____

_____

_____

_____

_____

_____

_____

Homework/Things to reflect on for next session:

_____

_____

_____

Post therapy:

Rate mood **after** session (circle):

————————	————————	————————	————————	————————
1	2	3	4	5
Sad/Down		Neutral/So-So		Happy/ Optimistic

What did you learn? Immediate thoughts after session:

_____

_____

_____

_____

_____

Reflection Page:

DATE: _____

_____

_____

_____

_____

_____

_____

_____

_____

_____

_____

_____

_____

_____

_____

_____

_____

_____

_____

_____

_____

_____

_____

_____

Session Date: _____

Rate mood **before** session (circle):

|———————|———————|———————|———————|
1   2   3   4   5
Sad/Down   Neutral/So-So   Happy/
                                      Optimistic

Session Notes: Jot down any words, topics, or notes from your therapy session.

_____

_____

_____

_____

_____

_____

_____

_____

_____

_____

_____

_____

_____

_____

_____

Homework/Things to reflect on for next session:

_____

_____

_____

Post therapy:

Rate mood **after** session (circle):

|—————|—————|—————|—————|
1   2   3   4   5

Sad/Down   Neutral/So-So   Happy/
                                                          Optimistic

What did you learn? Immediate thoughts after session:

_____

_____

_____

_____

_____

Reflection Page:

DATE: _____

_____

_____

_____

_____

_____

_____

_____

_____

_____

_____

_____

_____

_____

_____

_____

_____

_____

_____

_____

_____

_____

Session Date: _____

Rate mood **before** session (circle):

|————————|————————|————————|————————|
1   2   3   4   5

Sad/Down   Neutral/So-So   Happy/
Optimistic

Session Notes: Jot down any words, topics, or notes from your therapy session.

_____

_____

_____

_____

_____

_____

_____

_____

_____

_____

_____

_____

_____

_____

_____

_____

Homework/Things to reflect on for next session:

_____

_____

_____

Post therapy:

Rate mood **after** session (circle):

```
|—————————|—————————|—————————|—————————|
1          2          3          4          5
Sad/Down              Neutral/So-So              Happy/
                                                Optimistic
```

What did you learn? Immediate thoughts after session:

_____

_____

_____

_____

_____

Reflection Page:

DATE: _____

_____

_____

_____

_____

_____

_____

_____

_____

_____

_____

_____

_____

_____

_____

_____

_____

_____

_____

_____

_____

_____

_____

_____

_____

Session Date: _____

Rate mood **before** session (circle):

|————————|————————|————————|————————|
1   2   3   4   5
Sad/Down   Neutral/So-So   Happy/
                                         Optimistic

Session Notes: Jot down any words, topics, or notes from your therapy session.

_____

_____

_____

_____

_____

_____

_____

_____

_____

_____

_____

_____

_____

_____

_____

Homework/Things to reflect on for next session:

_____

_____

_____

Post therapy:

Rate mood **after** session (circle):

| _____ | _____ | _____ | _____ |
1   2   3   4   5
Sad/Down   Neutral/So-So   Happy/
Optimistic

What did you learn? Immediate thoughts after session:

_____

_____

_____

_____

_____

Reflection Page:

DATE: _____

_____
_____
_____
_____
_____
_____
_____
_____
_____
_____
_____
_____
_____
_____
_____
_____
_____
_____
_____
_____
_____
_____
_____
_____

Session Date: _____

Rate mood **before** session (circle):

|—————|—————|—————|—————|
1   2   3   4   5
Sad/Down   Neutral/So-So   Happy/
                                                     Optimistic

Session Notes: Jot down any words, topics, or notes from your therapy session.

_____

_____

_____

_____

_____

_____

_____

_____

_____

_____

_____

_____

_____

_____

_____

_____

Homework/Things to reflect on for next session:

_____

_____

_____

Post therapy:

Rate mood **after** session (circle):

| _____| _____| _____| _____|
1   2   3   4   5
Sad/Down   Neutral/So-So   Happy/
                                                 Optimistic

What did you learn? Immediate thoughts after session:

_____

_____

_____

_____

_____

Reflection Page:

DATE: _____

_____
_____
_____
_____
_____
_____
_____
_____
_____
_____
_____
_____
_____
_____
_____
_____
_____
_____
_____
_____
_____
_____
_____
_____

Session Date: _____

Rate mood **before** session (circle):

|————————|————————|————————|————————|
1   2   3   4   5
Sad/Down   Neutral/So-So   Happy/
Optimistic

Session Notes: Jot down any words, topics, or notes from your therapy session.

_____

_____

_____

_____

_____

_____

_____

_____

_____

_____

_____

_____

_____

_____

_____

Homework/Things to reflect on for next session:

_____

_____

_____

Post therapy:

Rate mood **after** session (circle):

|———————|———————|———————|———————|
1　　　　　　　2　　　　　　　3　　　　　　　4　　　　　　　5
Sad/Down　　　　　　Neutral/So-So　　　　　　Happy/
　　　　　　　　　　　　　　　　　　　　　　Optimistic

What did you learn? Immediate thoughts after session:

_____

_____

_____

_____

_____

Reflection Page:

DATE: _____

_____

_____

_____

_____

_____

_____

_____

_____

_____

_____

_____

_____

_____

_____

_____

_____

_____

_____

_____

_____

_____

_____

Session Date: _____

Rate mood **before** session (circle):

|—————|—————|—————|—————|
1   2   3   4   5
Sad/Down   Neutral/So-So   Happy/
                                            Optimistic

Session Notes: Jot down any words, topics, or notes from your therapy session.

_____

_____

_____

_____

_____

_____

_____

_____

_____

_____

_____

_____

_____

_____

_____

_____

Homework/Things to reflect on for next session:

_____

_____

_____

Post therapy:

Rate mood **after** session (circle):

|—————|—————|—————|—————|
1   2   3   4   5
Sad/Down   Neutral/So-So   Happy/
                                     Optimistic

What did you learn? Immediate thoughts after session:

_____

_____

_____

_____

_____

Reflection Page:

DATE: _____

_____
_____
_____
_____
_____
_____
_____
_____
_____
_____
_____
_____
_____
_____
_____
_____
_____
_____
_____
_____
_____
_____
_____
_____
_____

Session Date: _____

Rate mood **before** session (circle):

|—————|—————|—————|—————|
1   2   3   4   5
Sad/Down   Neutral/So-So   Happy/
                                                    Optimistic

Session Notes: Jot down any words, topics, or notes from your therapy session.

_____

_____

_____

_____

_____

_____

_____

_____

_____

_____

_____

_____

_____

_____

Homework/Things to reflect on for next session:

_____

_____

_____

Post therapy:

Rate mood **after** session (circle):

|——————|——————|——————|——————|
1   2   3   4   5
Sad/Down   Neutral/So-So   Happy/
Optimistic

What did you learn? Immediate thoughts after session:

_____

_____

_____

_____

_____

Reflection Page:

DATE: _____

_____

_____

_____

_____

_____

_____

_____

_____

_____

_____

_____

_____

_____

_____

_____

_____

_____

_____

_____

_____

_____

_____

Session Date: _____

Rate mood **before** session (circle):

|——————|——————|——————|——————|
1   2   3   4   5
Sad/Down   Neutral/So-So   Happy/
                                                    Optimistic

Session Notes: Jot down any words, topics, or notes from your therapy session.

_____

_____

_____

_____

_____

_____

_____

_____

_____

_____

_____

_____

_____

_____

_____

_____

_____

Homework/Things to reflect on for next session:

_____

_____

_____

Post therapy:

Rate mood **after** session (circle):

|————————|————————|————————|————————|
1   2   3   4   5

Sad/Down   Neutral/So-So   Happy/
Optimistic

What did you learn? Immediate thoughts after session:

_____

_____

_____

_____

_____

Reflection Page:

DATE: _____

_____
_____
_____
_____
_____
_____
_____
_____
_____
_____
_____
_____
_____
_____
_____
_____
_____
_____
_____
_____
_____

Session Date: _____

Rate mood **before** session (circle):

|————————|————————|————————|————————|
1   2   3   4   5

Sad/Down   Neutral/So-So   Happy/
                                                   Optimistic

Session Notes: Jot down any words, topics, or notes from your therapy session.

_____

_____

_____

_____

_____

_____

_____

_____

_____

_____

_____

_____

_____

_____

Homework/Things to reflect on for next session:

_____

_____

_____

Post therapy:

Rate mood **after** session (circle):

|————|————|————|————|
1   2   3   4   5
Sad/Down   Neutral/So-So   Happy/
                                                                     Optimistic

What did you learn? Immediate thoughts after session:

_____

_____

_____

_____

_____

Reflection Page:

DATE: _____

_____

_____

_____

_____

_____

_____

_____

_____

_____

_____

_____

_____

_____

_____

_____

_____

_____

_____

_____

_____

_____

Session Date: _____

Rate mood **before** session (circle):

|————————|————————|————————|————————|
1   2   3   4   5
Sad/Down   Neutral/So-So   Happy/
Optimistic

Session Notes: Jot down any words, topics, or notes from your therapy session.

_____

_____

_____

_____

_____

_____

_____

_____

_____

_____

_____

_____

_____

Homework/Things to reflect on for next session:

_____

_____

_____

Post therapy:

Rate mood **after** session (circle):

———————	———————	———————	———————
1	2	3	4	5
Sad/Down		Neutral/So-So		Happy/
				Optimistic

What did you learn? Immediate thoughts after session:

_____

_____

_____

_____

_____

Reflection Page:

DATE: _____

_____

_____

_____

_____

_____

_____

_____

_____

_____

_____

_____

_____

_____

_____

_____

_____

_____

_____

_____

_____

_____

_____

_____

Session Date: _____

Rate mood **before** session (circle):

|—————|—————|—————|—————|
1   2   3   4   5
Sad/Down   Neutral/So-So   Happy/
                                                    Optimistic

Session Notes: Jot down any words, topics, or notes from your therapy session.

_____

_____

_____

_____

_____

_____

_____

_____

_____

_____

_____

_____

_____

_____

_____

_____

_____

Homework/Things to reflect on for next session:

_____

_____

_____

Post therapy:

Rate mood **after** session (circle):

|———————|———————|———————|———————|
1   2   3   4   5
Sad/Down   Neutral/So-So   Happy/
                                                   Optimistic

What did you learn? Immediate thoughts after session:

_____

_____

_____

_____

_____

Reflection Page:

DATE: _____

_____

_____

_____

_____

_____

_____

_____

_____

_____

_____

_____

_____

_____

_____

_____

_____

_____

_____

_____

_____

Session Date: _____

Rate mood **before** session (circle):

|—————|—————|—————|—————|
1   2   3   4   5
Sad/Down   Neutral/So-So   Happy/
Optimistic

Session Notes: Jot down any words, topics, or notes from your therapy session.

_____

_____

_____

_____

_____

_____

_____

_____

_____

_____

_____

_____

_____

_____

Homework/Things to reflect on for next session:

_____

_____

_____

Post therapy:

Rate mood **after** session (circle):

|————————|————————|————————|————————|
1   2   3   4   5
Sad/Down   Neutral/So-So   Happy/
                                                 Optimistic

What did you learn? Immediate thoughts after session:

_____

_____

_____

_____

_____

Reflection Page:

DATE: _____

_____

_____

_____

_____

_____

_____

_____

_____

_____

_____

_____

_____

_____

_____

_____

_____

_____

_____

_____

_____

_____

_____

_____

Session Date: _____

Rate mood **before** session (circle):

|——————|——————|——————|——————|
1   2   3   4   5

Sad/Down   Neutral/So-So   Happy/
Optimistic

Session Notes: Jot down any words, topics, or notes from your therapy session.

_____

_____

_____

_____

_____

_____

_____

_____

_____

_____

_____

_____

_____

_____

_____

_____

Homework/Things to reflect on for next session:

_____

_____

_____

Post therapy:

Rate mood **after** session (circle):

|—————|—————|—————|—————|
1   2   3   4   5

Sad/Down   Neutral/So-So   Happy/
                                                       Optimistic

What did you learn? Immediate thoughts after session:

_____

_____

_____

_____

_____

Reflection Page:

DATE: _____

_____

_____

_____

_____

_____

_____

_____

_____

_____

_____

_____

_____

_____

_____

_____

_____

_____

_____

_____

_____

_____

_____

Session Date: _____

Rate mood **before** session (circle):

|————|————|————|————|
1　　　　　2　　　　　3　　　　　4　　　　　5
Sad/Down　　　　Neutral/So-So　　　　Happy/
　　　　　　　　　　　　　　　　　　　Optimistic

Session Notes: Jot down any words, topics, or notes from your therapy session.

_____

_____

_____

_____

_____

_____

_____

_____

_____

_____

_____

_____

_____

_____

_____

_____

_____

Homework/Things to reflect on for next session:

_____

_____

_____

Post therapy:

Rate mood **after** session (circle):

|————————|————————|————————|————————|
1   2   3   4   5
Sad/Down   Neutral/So-So   Happy/
                                                              Optimistic

What did you learn? Immediate thoughts after session:

_____

_____

_____

_____

_____

Reflection Page:

DATE: _____

_____

_____

_____

_____

_____

_____

_____

_____

_____

_____

_____

_____

_____

_____

_____

_____

_____

_____

_____

_____

Session Date: _____

Rate mood **before** session (circle):

|——————|——————|——————|——————|
1   2   3   4   5
Sad/Down   Neutral/So-So   Happy/
                                                  Optimistic

Session Notes: Jot down any words, topics, or notes from your therapy session.

_____

_____

_____

_____

_____

_____

_____

_____

_____

_____

_____

_____

_____

_____

_____

Homework/Things to reflect on for next session:

_____

_____

_____

134

Post therapy:

Rate mood **after** session (circle):

```
 |—————|—————|—————|—————|
 1         2         3         4         5
Sad/Down        Neutral/So-So        Happy/
                                     Optimistic
```

What did you learn? Immediate thoughts after session:

_____

_____

_____

_____

_____

Reflection Page:

DATE: _____

_____
_____
_____
_____
_____
_____
_____
_____
_____
_____
_____
_____
_____
_____
_____
_____
_____
_____
_____
_____
_____
_____
_____
_____

Extra Reflection Pages

These are extra pages for you to use throughout your therapy experience so that you can reflect more if needed after sessions.

DATE: _____

DATE: _____

DATE: _____

DATE: _____

DATE: _____

DATE: _____

DATE: _____

DATE: _____

DATE: _____

DATE: _____

DATE: _____

DATE: _____

DATE: _____

DATE: _____

DATE: _____

170

DATE: _____

DATE: _____

DATE: _____

DATE: _____

DATE: _____

DATE: _____

DATE: _____

DATE: _____

DATE: _____

DATE: _____

DATE: _____

DATE: _____

DATE: _____

DATE: _____

DATE: _____

DATE: _____

DATE: _____